CRAVINGS

COOKBOOK 2020

CRAVINGS COOKBOOK 2020

Simple And Easy Cravings Recipes Cookbook For Quick And Smart People | Gain Energy While Enjoying Delicious Recipes (Healthy Eating on a Budget)

ALEXIS KAYLA

TABLE OF CONTENTS

Introduction

We all know that the myth that only pregnant women can have cravings is a lie. Anyone can have cravings, and we have all lived at a time when we would throw ourselves in an iron in an ice cream tub; or we have dreamed of eating chocolate of all flavors and nothing and nobody could stop you.

Cravings can come for any reason, and this includes our emotional state. However, if you feel you feel like a particular type of food or a group of foods, your body may have low levels of some nutrient, vitamins or minerals. Cravings could be an indication that your body is asking for something specific, but not always what we want has the nutrient that our body asks us.

Knowing what our cravings mean gives us a certain advantage, in addition to helping us control what we eat and eliminate low-nutritious foods from our diet. Eating between meals has partly a psychological component. Stress, loneliness, low levels of essential components such as serotonin or dopamine, low sugar levels or boredom make us eat between meals , and the worst thing is that we opt for 'empty' foods, high in caloric content and no nutrient

Your Cravings May Indicate That You Lack These Nutrients

Many times cravings are signs that you need nutrients. Your body tells you what you need, learn to listen to it!

We have all had desperate cravings to eat something. And many times that "something" is not very healthy to say. However, our body is asking for it, we realize: it is almost impossible to ignore its call.

Actually, what you need is to learn to understand your body, which can sometimes have a little trouble sending a clear signal of what it wants.

When you crave some food with despair, what your body is saying is that it lacks nutrients. And what you want to eat has, of course, but perhaps added to a lot of other things not so good for health.

So, if you understand what nutrients your body is asking for when you have cravings, you can solve it by eating something healthy.

CHOCOLATE CRAVINGS

If you want to eat chocolate too much, your body is asking for magnesium. This is a mineral that provides energy and dilates blood vessels for better circulation.

Chocolate has this mineral, and in this case if you want to get the craving as your body asks you can do it. Of course, always choosing dark chocolate, which has more cocoa and less sugar?

If you do not have dark chocolate at home, it is best to replace it with dried fruits, such as nuts or almonds, or seeds. Sunflower seeds are especially rich in magnesium.

THE CRAVINGS FOR BREAD

Sometimes you may feel crazy desire to eat a good portion of bread: fluffy and warm. While it is a delight, and a pleasure that you can take without too much guilt (if it is only a portion), the truth is that your body really needs are amino acids, some fiber, and energy.

That is, your body feels a bit weak and needs strength. One way to replace the bread to really fulfill the craving you have is to eat nuts, quinoa or egg.

CRAVINGS FOR SOMETHING FRIED

Those days that you die from eating junk food of the purest, in general it is because you are in need of fat.

Yes, you need fat. These provide energy, allow the development and brain activity, protect the organs by cushioning, transport vitamins, are part of the structure of all the cells of our body, among many other functions.

The point is that there are different types of fats, and as you can imagine, those that bring fried foods and food are not the best. Therefore, if you want something like that, you can stop it with foods rich in healthy fats, such as avocado, seeds, nuts and vegetables.

SWEET CRAVINGS

When you feel like eating sweet things, what your body is asking for is glucose. This is very important in order to survive, since it is the primary source of energy.

The sweets contain high doses of glucose, but so much that it has an inverse effect: the overdose of this nutrient makes it impossible to process it, which is as if we had not eaten it. With a difference: it accumulates in the form of fat.

So it is not a good idea to succumb to sweet cakes if you have this craving, it will not calm your true needs. The best thing in these cases is to resort to fruit, which in addition to glucose has fructose, antioxidants and other nutrients.

At any whim

A preventive measure that you can take at any whim, and even in those moments when you feel that you feel like eating something but do not know what, is to drink a glass of water.

As you know, our body needs large amounts of water, and most of us don't drink enough. According to some studies, 80% of people are usually dehydrated.

Many times when the body asks for water, it is confused with cravings. Therefore, drink a glass or two of water and wait a few minutes before eating. You will see that more than once you want to eat.

Losing Weight

Losing weight is not a thing that goes overnight; it is a process in which the results are not always as fast as we expect. You have to understand that miracle pills and products that promise quick results are even dangerous and all they do is stunt your metabolism and lose weight for a while so that you have a huge bounce later.

Start by knowing your body and follow this guide to lose weight step by step:

Guide to lose weight step by step

CALORIES PER DAY

Losing weight is just about balancing the calories you consume and those you burn. For example, 0.50 kg equals 3,500 calories, which means that if you burn 500 calories daily for 7 days, you will lose half a kilo in a week.

Lean on a nutritionist and a nutrition plan where you can count the points and have specialized help to count the calories you eat in each dish and those you burn with certain activities.

KEEP TRACK

Look at your results. You do not have to become obsessed, but you must keep a check that allows you to compare and verify the results, only then will you know if you are reaching your goal. You can take a small agenda where you write down the obstacles you consumed during the day or use an application to count the calories you burn.

But never stop eating! The average daily calorie intake for women is 2,000, but it depends on age, height and other factors such as daily activity. We must not starve, we must eat healthy.

MEASURE

In this guide to lose weight step by step, something very important is to eat using measures, cups, scoops, fists, etc. This will help you not to exceed the portions you should eat. For example a cup of fruits, a fist of almonds and a spoonful of chia. At first it will be a bit difficult to measure, but then you will get used to it and know exactly how much you need to eat from each food. Po example:

EAT 5 TIMES A DAY

To avoid that feeling of hunger that leads us to binge eating it is better not to spend many hours without food. Do not spend more than 4 hrs without eating. It is much better to eat small portions 5 times a day, than to make 2 or 3 very heavy meals.

On the other hand, if you skip meals, the metabolism slows down, so you know, 5 meals are your best option. For example:

9:00 am- Breakfast 12:00 am- Snack 3:00 pm- Food 6:00 pm- Snack 9:00 pm- Dinner

CHOOSE YOUR FOOD WELL

What takes your body the longest to digest and therefore will leave you more satisfied is protein, on your plate there must be at least a quarter of protein. Check these recipes with protein. Another room should be divided between simple carbohydrates and healthy fats. There you already have a half of the covered plate. The other half of the dish should be covered by complex carbohydrates, especially vegetables. This will give you a good idea of having a balanced plate and where are you getting your calories.

REDUCE CALORIES

You should not stop eating, so you can reduce your calories with small actions that will give great results, for example: stop drinking soda and flavored drinks and sugar. Put a slice of cheese on your sandwitch instead of two. Replace the sugar with stevia. Instead of using bread for your dish use rice pancakes.

PLAN

One of the most difficult things in this weight loss guide is dealing with hunger. To prevent a soda machine, chips or a cookie from crossing your path, plan your meals and snacks for the week. If you're hungry, take a small fruit snack with you and avoid buying some donuts.

MOVE ON

Nutrition is one part of the process to achieve your goal. To lose weight you must include in your life the exercise. To burn calories and fat you must do cardio exercise for at least 30 minutes daily. It would be best if you did 60 minutes of cardio and a strength routine. Although the time you walk, run, swim, or whatever you like best, it will depend on the calories you need to burn.

SET SMALL GOALS AND CELEBRATE THEM

Losing weight is a process, which is why it is a good idea to set small goals that take you to the final goal. That is why we are teaching you to lose weight step by step. Your patience and willingness deserves a celebration, find healthy ways to celebrate every time you meet a goal (you don't necessarily have to involve food) for example: give yourself a spa day or go to the theater with your best friend.

FORGET MYTHS

The first thing is to know that diets and stop eating are not the solution. Any product or food that seems extremely restrictive or unhealthy will never be a good idea. You should also know that once you have lost weight you cannot forget about exercise and good habits; Weight is something that is maintained and you must maintain a healthy lifestyle.

BE PATIENT

Don't give up because you don't see immediate results. Losing weight the right way is a process. To lose weights step by step you must be patient, when you despair remember the reason why you are doing this. The effort will have a great reward.

Follow these tips to lose weight step by step and put on those jeans that you liked so much or take out the bikini that you stopped putting some time ago. Improve your life with healthy habits and sports a spectacular body.

As you will see, you do not need to starve yourself to lose weight; in fact you can achieve it by eating very well and very rich. The trick is knowing what nutritious foods to eat and how much to eat.

Cravings During Pregnancy

What do pregnant women crave? We have done a survey among BabyCenter users and we have discovered that most (almost 40 percent) want something sweet. A little less (33 percent) prefer salty foods. Fans of Mexican food and other spicy cuisines are in third place (17 percent). Behind them (10 percent) are those who like citrus, green apples and other acidic flavors. What does this all mean? This is what experts say about the whims in the diet of pregnant women:

Cravings are part of pregnancy, this cannot be denied. About 85 percent of women say they crave at least one type of food during pregnancy. And not all these cravings belong to the food diet, nor are they a plate of taste for many...

What the surveyed moms have confessed is that they want pickles wrapped in cheese, Mexican sauce with spoonfuls and even the fat of the meat. And if you have to classify cravings for sweet, salty, spicy or acidic flavors, we don't know very well where to put the olives with cheesecake. Another future mom told us that she loved sandwich cookies, with cheese inside, but that after having her baby she couldn't even see them! Another mommy was obsessed with eggplant, especially pizza. And a part of our readers claimed to consume large amounts of ice during pregnancy, although they had never consumed it before.

Many of these cravings have incredible intensity. What causes cravings during pregnancy? Can they be hormones ... for a change?

It's possible, says Elizabeth Somer, author of Nutrition for a Healthy Pregnancy. The enormous hormonal changes that a woman goes through during pregnancy can have a very powerful impact on her senses of taste and smell. This would explain why women who are going through menopause, which also involves hormonal changes, also experience those cravings and rejections of certain foods. But really, says Somer, nobody knows what exactly causes cravings.

Some experts do not believe that cravings can simply be attributed to hormones. Ronald Chez, a professor of obstetrics and gynecology at the University of South Florida, indicates that pregnancy has a similar effect on the bodies of all women, while cravings vary greatly from person to person.

"Nobody really understands what causes these cravings," says Chez. "An absolute cause could not be established scientifically."

Do Cravings Respond To A Nutritional Deficiency?

Not everyone thinks the same about this issue. Some nutritionists and doctors believe that certain cravings may arise to compensate for a nutritional need, but others are not so sure.

For example, the desire to eat ice or foreign substances such as starch to wash clothes or cigarette butts (a condition called pica) has been linked to an iron deficiency, even though none of these products contain significant amounts of this mineral.

San Francisco midwife and herbalist Cindy Belew says there are other food cravings to pay attention to. For example, practitioners of alternative medicine believe that a vitamin B deficiency can trigger an intense desire to eat chocolate. Belew also believes that many of his patients need essential fatty acids in their diet, because when they start taking flax oil, their cravings disappear.

Similarly, a craving for red meat seems to be a very clear need for protein. And the reader, who consumed large amounts of peaches (peaches), might be looking for beta carotene for her body. Despite this, Somer does not see much relationship between the cravings of a pregnant woman and what her body needs.

"People believe that cravings are significant, but studies show that there is no link between those and nutritional requirements," he says. "If pregnant women wanted what their body needs, they would all eat more broccoli and less chocolate."

What Can You Do With Your Cravings For Pregnant?

In summary, the experts we have consulted agree that you should pay attention to cravings during pregnancy, savoring those that are healthy and looking for alternatives for those that are not.

"Most cravings and rejections for certain foods are more interesting than serious and in general can be satisfied, although in moderation," says Somer. "A healthy diet should be one that meets the emotional and nutritional needs of the pregnant woman, as well as her preferences." Recommends that future moms take their cravings with humor, rather than fighting them, eating, for example, frozen fat-free yogurt, instead of ice cream, which usually carries a lot of fat.

Other ways to reduce unhealthy cravings are: having breakfast every day (skipping breakfast can increase cravings), exercising, and making sure you have a lot of emotional support. This is especially important, says Somer.

"The emotions that accompany pregnancy can make you want to use food to calm you down, when in reality what you need is a hug," he adds.

Healthy substitutes for cravings for junk food

Many women have cravings during pregnancy. And although some are willing to eat broccoli, bananas or oatmeal, most have visions of ice cream and chocolate on their heads.

If your desire for sugar and fat is too strong to resist it, treat yourself from time to time. But try to control your cravings so that your baby gets all the nutrients it needs for its development. (If you got type 1 or type 2 diabetes or gestational diabetes, follow the diet your doctor recommendation)

Here Are Ways To Control Your Cravings Without Suffering Too Much

Eat breakfast every day: You will avoid attacks of morning cravings. An excellent combination: a boiled egg, an orange, a slice of whole wheat bread and a glass of milk.

Exercise regularly: Physical activity is excellent to stop hunger and distract you from your cravings. Exercising regularly (walking daily, for example) will also help you stay fit.

Be smarter than your cravings: Have healthy snacks on hand when you're hungry. If you get a hunger attack and you have nothing ready to eat, you could end up filling yourself with candy and other things you don't need.

Get emotional support: Pregnancy hormones can make you more vulnerable to mood swings. You could take refuge in food when what you really need is a chat with a friend or a quiet walk to relieve stress and frustration.

Get used to thinking of small portions: Eat a few teaspoons of ice cream instead of a full bowl, or a chocolate bar instead of a whole tablet.

Use healthy substitutes when you crave junk food: Look for options that satisfy your desires and also provide the nutrients that you and your baby need. Here are some suggestions:

Instead of	Proof
Frozen	Semi-skimmed frozen yogurt or semi-skimmed ice cream with low sugar, scraped or fruit slush.
Can of cola	Mineral water with fruit juice or a splash of lemon.
Pizza	Use Arabic bread or a whole wheat tortilla (or look for a pizza dough recipe with brown rice flour and flaxseed) and cover it with roasted vegetables, tomato slices or marinara sauce and some grated Parmesan cheese.
Donut (donut) or cupcakes	Slice of whole wheat bread with raisins and cinnamon or half a whole grain bagel with cream cheese and a little jam.
Slice of cake or cake	Banana bread with nuts, low-fat zucchini bread, or angel cake (sponge cake, cake) with fresh or frozen strawberries.
Cereals with a lot of sugar and low fiber	Wholegrain cereal or oatmeal with a little brown sugar and cinnamon,

	raisins or dried cranberries.
French fries	Baked potatoes or tortillas instead of fried, popcorn (fat free or popcorn seasoning) or pretzels. Cut some tortillas or whole wheat bread in tortilla chips, sprinkle them with olive oil, sprinkle them on top with some herbs and bake them. Try baking pieces of cabbage, broccoli, cauliflower or chickpeas until they are crispy.
Cream	Semi-skimmed cream or plain yogurt.
Beef Burger	Portobello mushroom burger in a brown bread, with tomato or barbecue sauce and a slice of provolone cheese.
Fried chicken	Baked chicken, breaded with oatmeal or ground pretzels.
French fries	Sweet potato strips (sweet potatoes, sweet potatoes) or baked carrots.
Syrups and sweets to put on top of ice cream	Strawberries, raspberries, blackberries, sliced banana or chopped pineapple, with grated coconut or chopped nuts on top.
Canned fruit in syrup	Fresh fruit or frozen or canned fruit without sugar.
Chocolate	Cocoa prepared with skim or semi-skim milk. Or prepare a mixture of raisins, dried fruits, nuts and a handful of chocolate chips.
Biscuits	Integral cookies (Graham), ginger

	and other cookies with low sugar (if you want, use some peanut butter).
Cheesecake or other creamy dessert	Thin slices of cheese in whole wheat crackers, vanilla pudding or semi-skimmed rice pudding, or a little cream cheese with a little fruit jam on a whole wheat cookie.

Weight loss diets

Obesity is an excess of accumulation of fat in the body, greater than 25% in men and 33% for women. The location of this excess fat in the body can be a risk factor for the development of other diseases. Particularly, abdominal fat, common in men and women inside the menopausal phase, can favor the growth of hyperglycemia (high blood sugar levels), hypertension including alterations in cholesterol and the triglyceride levels.

Above all, obese people with respect to those who are not are at a high risk of suffering from the cardiovascular diseases, heart and respiratory failure, diabetes mellitus, high blood pressure, gallstones and colon cancer, among others.

To lose weight, you have to take into account multiple factors

In the latest position of the Spanish Society for the Study of Obesity (SEEDO) of 2016 entitled "Prevention, Diagnosis and Treatment of obesity" speaks of obesity as "a multifactorial disease where unthinkable protagonists have been added until a few years ago" . Overweight or obesity depends not only on what we eat but on many other factors such as physical activity, stress, intestinal microbiota (bacterial flora of the intestine), socioeconomic factors or the obesogenic environment that surrounds us.

It is clear that having excess fat in our body is not just a matter of what we eat. Being aware of the factors that affect each person allows us to better address the prevention and treatment of obesity.

The environment does not favor losing weight

The incidence of overweight and obesity in both adults and children does not stop growing. More and more people suffer and it seems that this trend will not change in the coming years. In fact, the World Health Organization does estimate that by 2030, 58% of Spaniards will be overweight and 21% obese. That said, it is clear that we are doing something wrong, without going any further around us.

We live in an obesogenic environment, that is, in an environment where there are a lot of factors that, without realizing it, bring us to overweight and obesity, conditioning our way of eating and our mobility.

And what are these factors? The 1 type of food that invades supermarkets, with a high energy density rich in sugars and unhealthy fats, 2 advertising and marketing that surrounds us and encourages us to buy certain products, the 3 social environment, the 4 automation of housework or the 5 availability of cars that reduce our physical activity.

Healthy food and physical activity, the keys to lose weight

Obesity is the result of many factors, and one of them is physical activity. Every time we move less. Office activities that keep us in a chair for 8 hours travel by car or motorcycle, technological advances that accommodate us (dishwasher, vacuum cleaner), lack of time and laziness to move.

Have you ever done the test to see how many steps you take per day? Do it and you will be surprised. And the worst part is that sometimes we spend the weekend on the couch because we want to rest.

How to get away from sedentary lifestyle? Take advantage of the trips to walk or go by bike, take the stairs at home, work and the subway, get off one or two stops before your destination and finish the journey walking. 2 days a week practice some sport or activity that you like as dance classes, hiking, bike rides on the weekend or a swimming course.

Physical exercise will make you feel better physically and psychologically and will be an aid to your goal of losing weight.

Take care of yourself without giving up your social life

Caring for your diet to lose weight does not mean neglecting the social life you share with your family and friends. If you think it is best to stay home and say no to the proposals you have to go out and enjoy you are wrong. That is not just sustainable over time and that can cause sadness, discouragement including anxiety. You must then learn to enjoy without compromising your goals. Take the healthiest options you have at your fingertips, moderate the amounts, know how to say "no" without fear and not fall into the error of compensating excesses with fasting or other behavior. Changing your behavior in these kinds of situations will help you maintain a healthy weight for a longer time.

Let nothing spoil your goal

Emotions are closely linked to how we eat. Sadness, happiness, stress, anxiety or boredom can make you take refuge in food as your escape valve consuming more fatty foods rich in sugar, snack between meals or binge losing control.

It seems that the solution is simple, don't do it. Even your family will have ever told you "if you know you need to lose weight, stop itching." You also have it clear, the theory you know but putting it into practice is very complicated.

In this sense it is essential to take care of sleep sleeping at least 7-8 hours a day, play sports, apply relaxation techniques such as yoga and lead a life as orderly as possible with regular schedules and planned meals.

Diets to lose weight

If you have come here, you have been thinking about how to go on a diet for a while. That is why here you will find all the information to be able to take action according to what your objective is.

Example of weekly weight loss diet

Below I have prepared an example diet that may be worth your reference. I have not put specific amounts of food because depending on your height, your current weight and your physical activity, these may vary. Also included is a space to the right where to point the shopping list. You can print this image and paste it in your fridge to serve as a guide. Remember that the ways of cooking are very important and try not to use more than two tablespoons of oil at each meal if you are a person over 40 years old and sedentary.

Breakfasts and dinners to lose weight

The two meals of the day that are usually more complicated are breakfast and dinner. The first because we usually have little time and the food industry has created many products very fast to consume, tasty but of a very low nutritional quality. Throughout our lives, advertising in this industry has told us how we have to have breakfast and we have to unlearn many years of misinformation.

On the other hand, the moment of family dinners usually takes us tired with what we eat the first thing we catch. So we have another article ready with ideas for quick dinner to lose weight.

Keys To Losing Weight Beyond Diet

The change that will allow you to lose weight without regaining weight

Overweight or obesity is a situation that develops due to numerous factors. The type of food, sedentary lifestyle, emotional aspects, and the state of health or the environment that surrounds us are just some of these factors that can trigger it.

If you need to lose weight, following a diet is not the solution (at least the only one). Don't consider taking care of yourself for a few months, taking medications, nutritional supplements or meal replacement for weight loss. Go to a nutritionist who treats your case in a personalized way, who teaches you to eat, buy and cook healthy. In short, improve your habits.

Stay away from sedentary lifestyle. Include walking walks and stairs in your daily routine. Practice some type of physical exercise that makes you enjoy (swimming, dancing, hiking ...)

Do not think that losing weight is going hungry, suffering and giving up eating a plate of pasta, a slice of bread or a banana. If you think that is because you have not found the right professional.

You have to know that a nice long road ahead awaits you since losing this excess weight will allow you to gain health and enjoy much more of various aspects of your life and your environment.

By getting your healthy weight back , you can achieve important day-to-day goals such as: improving your mobility and agility, being able to walk for a long time without getting tired, playing ball with your children or nephews, looking better physically, putting on clothes that you liked it and it has been a long time since you feel good.

In addition, from the point of view of health, the risk of chronic diseases such as heart disease, the type 2 diabetes, high blood pressure, strokes, infertility, sleep apnea, endocrine tumors or osteoarthritis, all are reduced. They, diseases that are exacerbated as the level of obesity increases.

To carry out a successful weight reduction program, you must integrate the consumption of healthier foods, physical exercise and the modification of important aspects of lifestyle.

And you, what do you want to lose weight for? It is possible to move from disorderly and inappropriate habits to more orderly and healthy ones that allow you to improve your quality of life.

How Long Can I Take To Lose 20 Kg?

The answer to this question has many variants depending on the type of diet you carry out. Surely you have heard of promises that ensure you lose 20 kg in 3 months , but do you really think they are healthy or rather they are miracle diets ?

A drastic decrease in calories that causes rapid weight reduction causes you to lose more muscle and water and can cause vitamin and mineral deficits.

In addition, poorly planned weight loss diets can cause hunger, bad mood, apathy, discouragement and anxiety. Many, because they eliminate basic foods that help improve your mood, such as bread or other cereals. Yes, the bread. It has been shown that weight loss diets that include this group of foods are better carried and the result is more lasting over time.

The gradual weight loss over a period longer helps reduce fat reserves, limits the loss of muscles and helps control the decrease in metabolic rate basal accompanying the rapid reduction in weight, i.e. reduces the tendency of Our body adapt to reducing calorie intake, spending less energy. Because eating "little" can also promote weight gain. Have you ever heard, "with what little I eat, I don't know why I am with this weight"?

According to scientific studies, a limitation of calories that causes a reduction of 0.25 to 0.5 kg per week in BMI of 27 to 35 and 0.5 to 1 kg in BMI> 35 is ideal to be able to maintain the weight achieved and avoid the rebound effect.

Therefore, we could say that for you to get an idea, you can lose 20 kg in about 10 months.

Will The Diet Be Sufficient?

To lose 20 kilos, you cannot simply adopt correct eating habits and not change anything else in your life.

Important aspects such as sleep, stress and physical activity are essential to achieve this goal. All of them are interconnected and when one of them is ignored, you can sabotage the rest.

- Sleep: Lack of sleep disrupts the mechanisms of endocrine regulation of hunger and appetite. Hormones that modulate appetite take a predominant role and may favor excessive energy intake. You must ensure that you sleep between 7-8 hours a day.
- Stress: Stress causes a release of adrenaline and cortisol, in a "fight or flight" response and has effects on the metabolism. As a consequence of this, the appetite is altered, being able to decrease or increase, but generally increases. In addition, a situation of stress or anxiety maintained over time can make weight loss difficult.

Therefore, we will need to find a way to manage that stress with activities that you like, such as painting, sewing, listening to music, yoga classes, and in general, enjoying your free time.

- Physical Activity: this is a key aspect to promote weight loss over time. If you are or have been sedentary all your life, it is important that you start with small steps such as walking to all the places you can instead of using the car; climb stairs, leaving the elevator aside; and mark you walking challenges to start.

For example, you can start by walking 30 min daily and write down the kilometers you do. The next week, the ride time increases. On the other you can try to do the same route, in a lower time and start jogging and thus leaving small goals progressively.

The practice of physical activity increases your daily caloric expenditure and in this way, helps the loss of body fat to work properly. In addition, as we always say, the diet should serve to change habits, and this is essential to ensure a better state of health.

What kind of diet to lose 20 kilos should I follow?

A balanced diet with energy restriction is the most reliable method to achieve long-term weight reduction.

Obviously, it is about carrying out a change of eating habits that not only serve to achieve the goal, but serve forever.

The low-calorie diet has to be individualized by your dietitian-nutritionist.

The most advisable decrease in calories is one that involves a reduction of 500 to 1000 kcal per day and its energy distribution is the following for a classic hypocaloric diet: includes carbohydrates at least in the three main meals (breakfast, food and dinner) trying to make most of them integral. Reduce your usual ration but do not eliminate cereal intake. Vegetables and fruits should be present ensuring 250-300g of vegetables per day and 300-350g of fruit per day. It is important that the protein intake comes from low-fat meats, fish and shellfish, eggs, low-fat dairy (fresh cheeses better than cured) or from plant-based foods such as legumes, nuts, seeds, soy and derivatives. Hecaloric intake in the form of fats should not exceed

30% of total calories. That 30% is reached very easily so we recommend: control the oil of your dishes! It is very healthy, but you should use it sparingly and avoid fried, battered and very heavy stews.

Key aspects to consider

1. Make the 5 daily meals: Eating every 3-4 hours will allow you to regulate blood glucose levels well and thus arrive well at the next meal to choose the healthiest foods that will make up your plate.
2. Drink like 1.5 and 2 liters of water daily. Broths and infusions also count as such. Avoid sugary and alcoholic drinks, since they add sugars and many daily calories to your diet.
3. Respect the idea of the dish. Your plate at lunch and dinner should bring vegetables, cereals or foods rich in carbohydrates and food Half of the meal will be based on vegetables or salads to provide satiety and low caloric value and thus regulate the subsequent consumption of more caloric foods such as those of protein origin and carbohydrates.
4. What is one of the simplest methods to feel full faster? Replace refined grains with whole grains rich in fiber and protein. But don't just change the white wheat bread for the wholegrain one day. Normally, these versions of whole wheat have only a negligible increase in fiber, and most have the same number of calories as refined ones. You will get the most fiber (and nutrients) when you eat intact whole grains, such as brown rice, whole wheat, legumes, quinoa and oats, among others.
5. Use varied cooking, but low fat, how: boiled, steam, iron, wok papillote, oven or stews with little oil. Avoid fried and battered.
6. Vary your dishes and use different ingredients and preparations, this way you will avoid monotony. It's about enjoying!
7. You can use all kinds of spices and herbs to flavor the dishes. Moderate the salt.
8. Chew food well and eat slowly to give time to feel the signs of satiety.

What Do I Do When I Have Holidays Or Celebrations Through?

During the time in which you will be with this loss of 20 kilos of weight there will be celebrations such as the chestnut, Christmas, Easter, family meals or with friends.

Are you worried about these situations? You do not know how to deal with them?

At this time, the consultation will help you, together with your nutritionist, to work these celebrations in advance so that when they appear, you can be more effective with sufficient resources. In addition, you can get healthier tips, ideas and recipes to be able to propose them and thus avoid making very caloric meals.

You have to be aware that you can enjoy social life like the rest, always trying to choose your diet in the healthiest way possible within your means.

Obviously when it's time for chestnuts, panellets, cannelloni or nougat you can afford to eat them, like everyone else. Of course, taste it in small portions, without stuffing yourself. The control will allow you to follow a good weight loss line.

What Happens If I Breathe And Stay?

You are in a process of change and as such, it is likely that along the way some relapse may occur.

A crucial aspect that can help you achieve the ultimate goal is to break down that goal into smaller goals that do not involve tremendous effort. Short-term goals make you gain confidence and motivation as you reaches them.

It may happen that the loss of the first kilos is easier because the level of motivation is very high and after a while, has decreased.

When you have been with the diet for a while, different emotions may appear such as boredom, anger or anger, anxiety. But the most important thing is to learn to regulate them.

Guilt may appear if one day you enter a pastry shop and you have not been able to resist eating chocolate croissants until you can no longer. Then there can be whipping thoughts how. What have you done? How could you theoretically you feel guilty because you made a mistake. Understand it as part of the process and take measures so that it does not happen again.

If you are anxious, check if you are eating in an orderly manner, if you are respecting the idea of the dish and you are not missing any food groups.

You may feel angry or angry because you are going to eat outside and it turns out that everyone is eating caloric and fatty dishes that seem appetizing and you choose healthier options to continue with your goal. In those moments you feel anger and envy because the rest of the table are thin and you think that they do not need to monitor what they eat ... But you will feel better if you think about the positive aspects that you are getting by reducing your weight.

It is possible that the time comes that you think the sacrifice is no longer worth it. What to do then?

At this point it could be time to redefine the objectives and assess whether you want to continue with weight loss or not. To do this, It's recommended that you ask yourself why you want to lose weight 20 kg and make a list of all of them. This will allow you to assess and become aware of the importance of the initial objective.

In consultation you can work on the rethinking of these objectives along with the barriers and resources that you have around you. Learning to identify the barriers that are presented to you both in the approaches, emotions, planning or in your environment, will help you anticipate these complicated situations, to know how to deal with them and manage them in the best possible way.

If you decide to resume weight loss again, it is important that you consider what has worked for you so far, what you have not tried yet, what you can do differently.

At this moment, your nutritionist can help you to promote creativity, to incorporate new things into your diet, new recipes, new ways of cooking, how to plan. Summing up, to vary both foods to choose how to cook them and their texture and presentation. And they don't have to be very complicated, elaborate and time-consuming recipes. You will be surprised how easy it is to cook fun and healthy in a short time.

For example, if we choose pumpkin, we can eat it in many ways:

- Pumpkin cooked inside a fresh salad with cherry tomatoes, marinated salmon, arugula and cucumber.
- Sliced pumpkin as a base and with a sea bass on top, baked.
- Pumpkin wok with other vegetables such as eggplant, pepper, mushrooms and accompanying a brown rice, for example.
- Cooked and kneaded pumpkin preparing a vegetable base to make a baked pizza.
- Pumpkin in cream.

- Pumpkin in papillote with mushrooms, spices and salmon.

That you don't like broccoli? have you tried steaming it and making it more consistent? Steamed vegetables have more flavors and you can vary their texture according to your tastes.

Do you think you'll get bored like that? We put the recipes and ideas, you will have to put your hands to elaborate it and then enjoy its flavor!

How To Prepare A Menu To Lose Weight

The shopping list has been organized by food groups to not forget anything:

VEGETABLES

Fresh vegetables: Onion, tomato, zucchini, eggplant, carrot, squash, broccoli, pepper, potato, lettuce, arugula, cucumber, sprouts, radishes.

Canned: corn, asparagus and palmitos.

PROTEIN

- Chicken: 2 days
- Golden / sea bass: 1 day
- Hake: 1 day
- Salmon: 1 day
- Egg: 3 days
- Veal: 1 day
- Legume: chickpeas 2 days and lentils 2 days

CARBOHYDRATES

- Rice
- Bread
- Couscous
- Potato
- Pasta

MONDAY

- Food
- First course

Baked vegetables. We have chosen pepper, pumpkin, whole tomato and broccoli (spices) We cut the vegetables into slices, add salt and spices. Keep in mind that you must make enough quantity for at least 3 days. Do not worry because once done it is preserved very well in the refrigerator all week, in a closed tupper to avoid cross contamination.

MAIN COURSE

Marinated chicken. Chop the chicken breasts and leave them macerating with lemon juice, oregano, parsley and salt for 12-24 hours. It will only be grilled at the time of eating. We add the carbohydrate that we will have prepared, in this case whole wheat pasta.

Puree dinner, which we have already done for several days. It is zucchini, onion and carrot but you can choose the vegetables that you have in the fridge. We accompany this mashed tortilla roll with vegetables. To do this you make a finite tortilla in a large pan and roll it with chopped tomatoes, lettuce and grated carrots. Accompanied with whole wheat bread.

TUESDAY

Food

Salad (I) with lettuce, tomato, arugula, cucumber, corn and palmettos. As we want a unique dish, we add the lentils that you have previously cooked or preserved, washing and draining. And brown rice that we will also have cooked.

Baked vegetables, same as Monday and baked sea bass or sea bream with potato chips. You can cook fish and potatoes at the same time. Cut the finite potatoes with a mandolin, wash them to remove excess starch, dry them, add a little oil and spices and put everything on the tray with baking paper.

WEDNESDAY

Puree food, such as Monday night and grilled salmon, or if you prefer steamed or papillote.

Dinner

Salad (I) of lettuce, tomato, arugula, cucumber, corn and palmettos. Marinated chicken that we prepared on Monday. The carbohydrate that will accompany dinner will be couscous, which you can have done but you can also prepare it at the time. Simply hydrate it by putting the same volume of water or hot broth as couscous, let it hydrate and go.

THURSDAY

Food On

Thursday, we finish our baked vegetables and accompany them with hake and couscous the night before. The hake can be cooked on the grill or in the microwave or papillote.

DINNER

Ratatouille with crushed tomatoes, zucchini, eggplant and onion. As we talk about a weight loss menu, you have to moderate the use of oil. For example in this case we will cook the vegetables over low heat and cover to take advantage of the broth that the vegetables are releasing. Once the ratatouille is made, we add the chickpeas as a protein ration and the potato that you will have cooked or you can even do it at the time in the microwave.

FRIDAY

Food

We will eat the ratatouille that has been left over from the previous night but this time accompanied by veal and mixed with brown rice. For those who eat tupper, you can prepare the veal chopped and shaped like a hamburger. Make sure it's 100% lean veal.

DINNER

Salad (II) with sprouts (canons, arugula), asparagus, carrots, radishes, cherry tomatoes. Poached egg and whole wheat bread. Here you have the poached egg recipe:

To make the egg poche you need a small bowl or a cup. Cut a piece of transparent film that is larger than the container, enough to wrap the egg and make a sack. Then pour the egg and season to taste, with a pinch of salt is enough. Close the bag. Heat water in a casserole and when it starts to boil add the sack with the egg. In 4 minutes it will be cooked.

SATURDAY

Food

We will have dinner the salad (II) of the previous night and tuna marmitako. The recipe marmitako is this:

Ingredients : Nice without skin or thorns, diced, 1 large potato, 1 onion, 3 tomatoes, ½ green pepper, garlic, olive oil, salt and pepper

Preparation: Peel and chop the garlic, onion and pepper. Fry it with a little olive oil. Add the natural crushed tomato and after 5 minutes, toss the diced potato, the fish stock (or failing that of vegetables) until the potato is covered and let it simmer until the potato is tender. Sprinkle the tuna and add it to the stew. After 5 minutes, turn off the heat and cover, let it finish cooking with the residual heat.

Puree dinner (third and last day in which we include this preparation). We will add the chickpeas on the mash as if they were croutons of bread. To do this you must toast the chickpeas in the oven or in the pan so that they are crispy. Grilled cuttlefish with garlic and parsley.

SUNDAY

Food

Very simple salad with chopped ripe tomato, ½ avocado and lentils (which we will boil or canned) and brown rice.

Pisto dinner (which we will have done) Grilled egg: very simple. In a nonstick skillet, put a few drops of oil, put the egg, cover it and let it cook over medium heat until the clear set and the yolk is liquid, to wet with the bread and suck your fingers.

THE PROTEIN IN THE WEIGHT LOSS MENU

At the moment we left the proteins. Although we could leave them done if we have cooked stews or baked in our menu we have decided to make them at the time. If you have them defrosted in the fridge in 2-3 minutes you can cook them. As you can see we have the macerated chicken that we cook on the grill and also the salmon and the veal, we have an omelet and a grilled egg, a baked sea bass and the microwave hake.

According to the latest 2016 guidelines, an omnivorous person who wants to follow a balanced diet can follow the following weekly protein consumption frequencies:

2-4 weekly portions of white fish, 2-4 weekly portions of white meat, 2-4 weekly portions of eggs, 1-2 weekly portions of blue fish, 2-3 weekly portions of legumes and between no and 1 serving of meat red They are frequencies designed for an omnivorous person, of course.

In a menu to lose weight or lose weight, in addition to lunch and dinner the rest of the meals must be healthy. Breakfasts, lunches and snacks that include foods such as fruits, whole wheat bread or other cereals such as oatmeal, skimmed milk if we talk about weight loss diet and small portions of nuts.

Cleansing the Body of Harmful Things

Keeping your body clean, that's important, not only to prevent the onset of many illnesses but to feel healthy and beautiful and have the ideal weight. And what could be better for cleansing the body than vegetables and fruits, proper use can be the best way to maintain health and beauty, as the body deserves.

General information

1. All fruits and vegetables should be of the highest quality, preferably organic.

2. Always wash fruits and fruits well.

3. Not much seasoning or sweet.

4. Make sure your vegetables are always eaten as fresh as possible.

5. A cleansing diet usually causes symptoms such as abdominal pain, diarrhea, nausea, and so on. This is normal because in the process of cleansing these reactions can be in the body. However, you should not give up the diet unless the symptoms are very pronounced and unusual. In this case, visit a naturopath or the health service.

6. If you drink juice, avoid sifting, drink slowly and chew. This is great for body cleansing.

Self-cleaning of the organism

This happens through the five organs that are there, namely kidneys, liver, intestine, lungs, and lymph. Detoxification mechanisms of the human body work well when the conditions are very good, which means that there is no increased uptake of toxins from food, water, and air. Stress and lack of physical activity contribute to the weakening of these natural functions of the organism.

The winter time is marked by holidays, which result in some extra pounds. They are one of the motivators to accelerate your metabolism through high-quality detoxification and promote weight loss. It is essential to emphasize that detoxification is not a slimming method but can be stimulating because it positively affects metabolism. There are also many infections that we are more prone to in winter. The detoxification helps the organism to cope with viruses and bacteria more easily because it is not pre-loaded with waste.

During a diet change, when a healthy diet is required, it is recommended to detoxify the organism, which prepares the digestive tract for better nutrition to better absorb the nutrients. The natural detoxification is particularly suitable for seasonal changes. Especially if you recognize the signals of the organism that it is loaded with certain substances and should be cleaned.

It uses foods that are high in fiber and have a diuretic effect to accelerate digestion and cleanse the gastrointestinal tract.

Study on how fruits and vegetables affect the purification of the organism

A study published in the American National Institute of Health (NIH) found that increased consumption of basic fruits and vegetables can reduce the acidity of the blood and help the body with detoxification. When blood toxins arrive in the liver, "allies" are needed to filter out all harmful substances and protect the body from the disease. These allies are fresh fruits and vegetables, especially green and red.

Some other phenomena may indicate that we have a problem with accumulated toxins. This is the appearance of pimples, skin problems, flatulence and gastrointestinal disturbances, bad breath, allergies, painful periods and lack of concentration. Of course, it is not necessary to wait for these symptoms to dedicate themselves to cleaning the body of toxins. The best way is to make a detoxification program seasons and thus keep the organism fit.

How To Speed Up The Metabolism

If you're among those who struggle with excess pounds, you've probably already thought about how to speed up your metabolism significantly. Losing weight is unfortunately not simple math, according to which you have to take the appropriate number of calories that you consume in a day. The important thing is whether these calories come from fat, sugar, dough, or fruits and vegetables. Most vegetables have a lower calorie count, which means you can eat more and not gain weight. The particular advantage of using fruit and vegetable juices together with enough water is the acceleration of the metabolism. After a detox diet, the body usually loses several pounds.

Instead of allowing bacteria and viruses to run wild, we recommend that you do without foods containing many additives, colors, and preservatives. The next step, of course, is to cleanse the body to prevent the onset and development of the disease and regain energy. Fatigue and headaches will disappear first. New energy, a better mood and the feeling that there are no health problems make detoxification an unsurpassed method.

Obtained nutritional value of food

The inclusion of foods without thermal treatment sets us apart from other juice manufacturers. Only fruits and vegetables that are pressed under pressure with a hydraulic press make it possible to retain all the useful properties of juices. Juices are pressed without the influence of heat, which normally develops during normal squeezing, and without air supply (airtight), with the result that there is no oxidation process of fruits and vegetables. The extended shelf life of the juices is achieved only by the pressure generated by the hydraulic press. The fully preserved nutritional value of the food, without the addition of sugars and preservatives, can charge the organism with energy in the short term.

So, the juice you get stays fully intact until you open it. This is not possible in the supermarket, and it is very difficult to do that at home. We control the origin and freshness of ingredients very strictly. We receive them every morning from certified manufacturers who refrain from using chemicals in plant cultivation. In the production of juices, we combine modern technology of hydraulic presses and traditional handwork. And above all, we do what we like, and this brings success.

Here Are Lists Of The Recipes

Tasty Bbq Ribs

Preparation: 15 min

Cooking time: 4 h 5 min

This recipe is a delicious dish of Tasty BBQ Ribs so you can prepare your whole family as a main course. Accompany with a delicious salad and surprise them with these new flavors.

Ingredients

8 Servings

- 2 ribs racks of ribs
- 2 1/2 teaspoons brown sugars

- 1 1/4 teaspoons instant coffees
- 1 1/4 teaspoons kosher salt
- 1 1/4 teaspoons garlic powder
- 1 1/4 teaspoons coriander laces
- 3/4 teaspoon fine grounded black pepper special
- 1/4 of teaspoon of cocoa powder
- 1 teaspoon vegetable oil
- 1 1/2 cups dry red wine
- 2 tablespoons canola oil
- 2 tablespoons chopped white onion
- 2 cups of catsup sauce
- 1 1/2 cups apple cider vinegar
- 3/4 cup brown sugar
- 1 1/2 tablespoons of Maggi chicken broth
- 3 tablespoons Dijon mustard
- 2 teaspoons chili powder
- 2 teaspoons marinated chipotle chili sauce

Preparation

1. FOR THE RIBS:
2. Arrange the racks of ribs on a baking sheet with edges or inside a large roasting pan.
3. Using a knife, remove the membranes from the bone side of the ribs (this step is very important to make the ribs tender).
4. Dry the ribs with a paper towel; Place on the grill with the meat side facing up.
5. Combine the sugar, coffee granules, salt, garlic powder, coriander, pepper and cocoa in the spice grinder; Cover and process until smooth.
6. Lightly rub the ribs with oil.
7. Sprinkle with the mixture, pressing gently to support it adhere to the ribs.

8. Allow it stand at room temperature for no more than 1 hour.
9. Preheat the oven to 250 F. Pour the beer into the bottom of the baking sheet.
10. Cover the bowl with foil, bake for 4 to 5 hours (this will be enough to make the meat tender, but it won't fall off the bones).
11. Prepare the BBQ sauce during the last 30 minutes of baking.
12. Preheat the grill.
13. Grill the ribs over medium heat, turning once, for 5 minutes. Spread with sauce during roasting. Allow the ribs stand for 10 minutes before serving.
14. FOR BBQ SAUCE:
15. Heat the oil in a medium saucepan on medium heat.
16. Put the onion and then cook for 3-5 minutes or until tender.
17. Add the catsup sauce, vinegar, sugar and broth. Stir until the sugar and the broth dissolve.
18. Add mustard, chili powder and marinade. Cover and cook for 30 minutes. The sauce will thicken as it simmers.

Nutritional information

- Percentage of daily values based on a 2,000 calorie diet.
- Calories 253 kcal 13%
- Carbohydrates 48.7g 16%
- Protein 1.6g 3.1%
- Lipids   3.8g 5.9%
- Dietary fiber   0.2g 0.5%
- Sugars 38.0g 42%
- Cholesterol   0.4mg 0.1%

Bourbon Barbecue Chops

Cooking time:1 h 30 min

The barbecue chops are a very tasty dish to watch a football game or for a barbecue. The barbecue bourbon chops recipe is a variation of the traditional recipe with a bourbon-type whiskey sauce.

Ingredients

- 6 Servings
- 1 kilo of beef chop
- 1/4 cup bourbon
- 4 tablespoons honey
- 3 tablespoons hoisin sauce
- 3 tablespoons tabasco sauce
- 2 tablespoons soy sauce
- 2 tablespoons Worcestershire sauce
- to taste of pepper to taste
- 2 cups pineapple juice

Preparation

1. Preheat the oven to 220 degrees Celsius.
2. Take the chops and season with salt and pepper. In two large baking sheets put two aluminum foil jars on them, inside which are the chops with pineapple juice. Bake for 1 hour.
3. While the chops are baking, prepare the charcoal and the sauce.
4. In a deep bowl, mix the bourbon, honey, hoisin sauce, Tabasco, soy sauce and English sauce.
5. Remove the chops from the oven and cut each rib in half. With a brush, paint the chops with the sauce and cook on the carbon (barbecue).
6. Cook for 2-3 minutes and change sides, repaint the chops every 3 minutes during cooking.
7. Cook to the desired term and serve.

Nutritional information

- Percentage of daily values based on a 2,000 calorie diet.
- Calories   592   kcal 30%
- Carbohydrates 22.6   g 7.5%
- Protein 50.8   g 102%
- Lipids   28.9   g 44%
- Dietary fiber   0.2   g 0.4%
- Sugars 20.7   g 2. 3%
- Cholesterol   197   mg 66%

Whole chicken grilled in a slow cooker

Servings: 4 to 6

Preparation time: 20 minutes

Cooking time: 8 hours at low intensity

Ingredients

- 1 lemon cut into quarters
- 1 stem of rosemary
- 1 stem of thyme leaves
- 1 whole chicken of 1.5 kg (3 1/3 lb)

For the dry marinade:

- 15 ml (1 tbsp.) Of paprika
- 15 ml (1 tablespoon) of onion powder
- 15 ml (1 tbsp.) Of brown sugar
- 15 ml (1 tbsp.) Of crushed coriander seeds
- 10 ml (2 tablespoons) of garlic powder
- Salt and pepper to taste

Preparation

1. Insert the lemon wedges and herbs into the chicken cavity. Tie the chicken.
2. In a bowl, combine the ingredients of the dry marinade. Rub the chicken with this preparation.
3. Form five balls with sheets of aluminum foil. Place the balls at the bottom of the slow cooker.
4. Place the chicken on the balls of aluminum foil to elevate it.
5. Cover and cook lightly for 8 to 9 hours.
6. When cooking is complete, preheat the oven to the "broil" position.
7. For baking, place the chicken on a baking sheet lined with aluminum foil and brown in the oven for 3 to 5 minutes. For barbecuing: place the chicken on the hot, oiled barbecue grill and cook for 12 to 15 minutes.

Cooking on the barbecue

1. Follow steps 1 to 5.
2. Preheat the barbecue to medium-high power.
3. Place the chicken on an aluminum tray.
4. On the hot barbecue grill, remove the aluminum tray. Close the lid and then cook for 12 to 15 minutes, until the skin of the chicken is crisp.

Nutritional information

- Per serving: 415 calories; 32 g protein; MG 36 g; carbohydrates 6 g; fibers 2 g; iron 3 mg; calcium 45 mg; sodium 127 mg

Baked sea bream in Lebanese style

Ingredients:

For the dish:

- 1 kilogram of whole fish type bream, salmon or trout
- 1 teaspoon of salt
- 1 teaspoon of cumin

- 1 teaspoon sweet pepper (paprikas)
- 1 onion
- 1 lemon
- 2 bay leaves
- 3 tomatoes
- For the sauce:
- 3 cloves of garlic
- 1 tablespoon coriander seeds
- 1/2 teaspoon of salt
- 100 g of onion
- 1/2 bunch of green coriander
- 65 g of tahini (sesame puree)
- 1 lemon or about 50 ml of lemon juice
- 1/2 glass of vegetable oil (sunflower or olive)
- 10 g pine nuts
- 25 g chopped walnuts
- 1/2 to 1 teaspoon of fine cayenne pepper powder (according to taste)
- 1 pinch of pepper

Preparation:

1. Wash the fish; rub both sides with a teaspoon of salt, sweet pepper, and cumin. In a large baking tray, add the onion, tomatoes, and lemon sliced and put the fish and bay leaf. Add 1 glass of water. Sprinkle with a drizzle of olive oil.
2. Heat up the oven to 180 ° C. Put the tray in the oven and cook for 20 minutes or 25 minutes depending on the type and thickness of the fish.
3. With a pestle, crush garlic, salt, and coriander seeds until coriander becomes powder. Set aside.
4. Minute an onion, finely chop green coriander and leave aside.

5. In a large bowl, pour tahini, lemon juice, and 100 ml water. Mix well until you obtain a homogeneous liquid, then reserve.
6. In a saucepan, add vegetable oil, heat over medium heat. Brown the pine nuts, drain them.
7. In the same saucepan and remaining oil, brown the chopped onion. Add green coriander, the garlic-cilantro mixture in seeds and chopped walnuts and pepper. Simmer another 10 minutes. Finally, add tahini, lemon, and water. Cook for about 10 minutes. 8. Add the chili, mix and remove from the heat. Leave this sauce aside for dressing.
8. To serve, place the fish on a large plate, decorate with slices of peppers, tomatoes or any other vegetable to give color. Put the sauce on the fish, and then scatter over the pine nuts.
9. Good realization and good tasting!

Nutritional Information

- Potassium 967.12mg   28%
- Carbohydrates 0g   0%
- Dietary Fiber 0g   0%
- Sugars 0g

Beef Dish with Bird Lettuce

Cooking time: More than 60 min

Ingredients

- Servings: 4
- 600 g boiled beef (cooked)
- 6 cl of Sherry Dry
- 2 carrots
- 2 turnips (yellow)
- 1/4 celeriac
- 4 tablespoons of chives (chopped)
- 600 ml of beef soup
- 10 sheets of gelatin
- Vegetable oil (for the form)
- Pepper (from the mill)

- Salt
- 200 g of bird's lettuce
- Pumpkinseed-pesto
- Chives (to sprinkle)

For The Marinade:

- 4 tablespoons of corn oil
- 3 tablespoons apple cider vinegar
- 2 tablespoons of beef soup
- Pinch of salt

Preparation

1. Boil the soup with 200 ml of water.
2. Add carrots, yellow turnips and celery and cook until soft. Remove from the soup, let cool and cut into 3 mm thick strips.
3. Soak the gelatin inside cold water, squeeze and add to the soup. Season well with sherry, salt and pepper and remove from Air fryer heat.
4. Spread the terrine mold with little oil, insert the plastic wrap lengthwise and smooth with kitchen paper.
5. Cut the top of the heated beef from the Air fryer (preferably with the bread slicer) into 2 mm thick slices, dip each slice into the still warm soup one at a time and line the shape with it. In doing so, arrange overlapping about 6 cm over the edge.
6. Pour in a little soup, sprinkle with chives, place the vegetable strips lengthways and top them dipped in soup. Repeat this process three times; Pour in the rest of the soup.
7. Press foil and refrigerate for 3 hours. For the marinade, mix all ingredients with a whisk and marinate the lettuce. Toss the terrine, remove the foil and cut into slices.

8. Arrange on chilled plates and garnish with the marinated lettuce. Drizzle with pumpkin seed pesto and sprinkle with chives.

Tip

- Depending on the season, the vegetable inlay of the Sulz can be modified with radishes, asparagus or pickled mushrooms. Drizzled with apple cider vinegar and sprinkled with Fleur de sel and pepper, the Sulz tastes even spicier.

Nutrition Information

- 221kcal
- Fat: 13g
- Saturated fat: 7g
- Carbohydrates: 1g
- Protein: 23g

Keto stuffed avocados with smoked salmon

2 portions

Ingredients

- 2 avocados
- 175 g smoked salmon
- 175 ml fresh cream or mayonnaise
- Salt and pepper
- 2 tbsps. lemon juice (optional)

Instructions

1. Slice the avocados into half and remove the bone.
2. Put a spoonful of fresh cream in the hollow of the avocado and add smoked salmon on top.

3. Season to taste with little salt and sprinkle with lemon juice to give more flavor (and avoid the avocado acquires a brown color).

Advice

- This ketogenic dish can be served with any other type of fatty fish, boiled, fried or smoked. It tastes better with a little fresh dill!

Salad with Avocado, Pineapple And Cucumbers

Time preparation: 25 min.

Servings: 4

Ingredients

- 1 sliced cucumber
- 3 slices of pineapple (pineapple)
- 1/2 red onion filleted
- 2 avocados (avocados)
- 1/3 cup olive oil
- 2 tbsp lemon juice
- 1 cdita salt
- 1 cdita pepper

Preparation

1. Cut the avocado and pineapple in medium cubes.
2. Subsequently cut the cucumber along, remove the seeds with a spoon and cut into slices.
3. Mix the above inside a bowl, add the red onion, salt, pepper and season with olive oil and lemon juice.

Nutritional information

- Calories: 90.2
- Total Fat: 4.6 g
- Dietary Fiber: 2.5 g
- Saturated Fat: 1.7 g

Mango and avocado salad

You will love the colors of this salad of mango, and avocado. The mixture makes it a vibrant and fun salad.

4 people

Time preparation: 10 minutes

Ingredients for 4 people

- 1 unit (s) of chopped Lettuce
- 1 pinch of Pepper
- 1 unit (s) of Avocado
- 1 unit (s) of Mango
- 1 tablespoon White wine vinegar
- 1 tablespoon of olive oil
- 2 tablespoon of chopped toasted almonds

- 2 tablespoon dried cranberries
- Salt

Preparation

1. Peel and chop the vegetables.
2. Put the lettuce, mango, avocado, almonds, and cranberries in a bowl.
3. On the other hand, mix the oil with the vinegar and add salt and pepper.
4. Pour over the salad and mix.
5. Serve on plates and enjoy.

Nutritional composition for 100 grs

- Composition   Amount (gr)   CDR (%)
- Kcalories   259.3   13.5%
- Carbohydrates   19.59   6.3%
- Proteins   4.15   8.7%
- Fiber   5.77   19.2%
- Fat   16.98   31.9%

Avocado and lettuce salad

2 people

Time preparation: 10 minutes

Ingredients for 2 people

- 1 unit (s) of Tomato cut
- 1 unit (s) of Lettuce
- 0.5 unit (s) of red pepper, diced julienne
- 1 pinch of Pepper
- 1 unit (s) of Avocado
- 2 tablespoon Nuez chopped (walnut crepes)
- 1 pinch of salt
- 2 tablespoon of Modena balsamic vinegar
- 2 tablespoon of lemon juice
- 1 pinch of extra virgin olive oil

Preparation

1. Wash the lettuce well and chop it.
2. Wash and chop the remaining ingredients such as the Tomato, red pepper or diced julienne, Avocado, Nuez chopped Modena balsamic vinegar.
3. Mix the lemon juice, vinegar, virgin oil, salt, and pepper. Then toss on the salad.
4. Remove and add the nuts (optional) to garnish.

Nutritional composition for 100 grs

- Composition   Amount (gr)   CDR (%)
- Kcalories   315.53   16.5%
- Carbohydrates   10.8   3.5%
- Proteins   6.55   13.7%
- Fiber   7.55   25.2%
- Fat   25.88   48.7%

Zucchini Spaghetti

1 person

Time preparation: 10 minutes

Ingredients for 1 person

- 1 unit (s) of zucchini
- 1 pinch of Herbamare herbal salt or normal salt

Preparation

1. Pass the zucchini ALONG by the large grater; nothing happens if it is cut in half because it is impossible to make it perfect.

2. When you have grated all the zucchini, Herbamare herbal salt or normal salt and prepare while your sauce so that the zucchini is losing water.
3. You can heat them in a pan, but raw tastes less and takes the flavor of what you throw to accompany.
4. Add the sauce with which you will combine it and serve it.

Nutritional composition for 100 grs.

- Composition   Amount (gr)   CDR (%)
- Kcalories   44.3   2.3%
- Carbohydrates   3.85   1.2%
- Proteins   3.58   7.5%
- Fiber   3.04   10.1%
- Fat   0.96   1.8%

Salad of red beans with guacamole

4 people

Time preparation: 30 minutes

Ingredients for 4 people

- 1 unit (s) of Tomato (medium)
- 1 unit (s) of Onion (half onion purple)
- 1 unit (s) of red pepper (medium)
- 1 pinch of Pepper
- 1 unit (s) of Limón
- 1 pinch of salt
- 1 unit (s) of Green pepper
- 250 grams of Azuki a pot (canned red beans already cooked)
- 1 tablespoon of extra virgin olive oil
- 1 unit (s) of fresh Guacamole Frutas Montosa (Mercadona) you can make it homemade too
- 1 small cup of sweet corn in a can

Preparation

1. Prepare the salad by mixing all the chopped ingredients such as Tomato, Onion, Limón, with the beans previously washed, Azuki and drained.
2. Dress with lemon juice and oil and season with salt and Green pepper.
3. Serve the salad with the guacamole and toast with toasted bread.

Nutritional composition for 100 grs.

- Composition   Amount (gr)   CDR (%)
- Kcalories   353.04   18.4%
- Carbohydrates   42.06   13.5
- Proteins   14.75   30.8%
- Fiber   13.82   46.1%
- Fat   10.33   19.4%

Vegetarian recipe

Time preparation: 1 hour

Ingredients:

- 1 cup of green beans
- 2 carrots
- Sweet corn
- Cooked rice
- A teaspoon of mustard
- A little honey
- Olive oil
- A handful of cooked chickpeas
- Three or four chopped pistachios

Preparations:

1. You have to mix some green beans and some boiled or steamed carrots, along with sweet corn and cooked rice.
2. To dress it, mix a teaspoon of mustard with a little honey and olive oil. And if you want to turn it into a complete and balanced single dish, you can add a handful of cooked chickpeas and three or four chopped pistachios. Besides being delicious, this vegetarian recipe is one of the best meals to take to work.

Nutritional information

- Calories: 111
- Total Fat: 2g
- Saturated Fat: 1g
- Cholesterol: 10mg
- Sodium: 58mg
- Carbohydrates: 19g
- Fiber: 0 g
- Sugar: 18 g
- Calcium: 15%
- Iron: 0%

Raw Vegetables. Chopped Salad

Preparation time: 15 minutes

Total time: 15 minutes

Ingredients

- Chopped raw veggie salad
- 1 orange pepper (minced) (about 1 cup)
- 1 yellow pepper (small cut) (about 1 cup)
- 5-8 radishes (halve and cut into thin slices) (about 3/4 cup)
- small head of broccoli (minced) (about 2 cups)
- 1 seedless cucumber (small cut) (about 2 cups)
- 1 cup of halved red seedless grapes
- 2-3 tablespoons chopped fresh dill

- 1/4 cup chopped fresh parsley
- 1/4 cup of raw peeled sunflower seeds
- 1/8 cup raw hemp hearts (peeled hemp seeds)
- Oil-free dressing
- garlic clove (chopped)
- tablespoons of red wine vinegar
- 1 tablespoon of apple cider vinegar
- Juice of 1 lemon
- 1 tbsp Dijonsenf
- 1 tbsp pure maple syrup
- 1/2 teaspoon salt (or to taste)
- 1/8 tsp pepper (or to taste)

Preparation

1. Whisk the ingredients - Chopped raw veggie salad, 1 orange pepper, yellow pepper, radishes, small head of broccoli, seedless cucumber, halved red seedless grapes, chopped fresh dill, chopped fresh parsley, raw peeled sunflower seeds, raw hemp hearts, garlic clove, red wine vinegar, apple cider vinegar, lemon, Dijonsenf, pure maple syrup, salt, pepper. For dressing inside a small bowl and set aside.
2. Combine all the salad ingredients in a large bowl.
3. Pour the dressing over the chopped vegetables then wrap well.
4. Cover and then refrigerate it for an hour or two and toss the salad once or twice during this time to coat evenly. Enjoy!

Notes on the recipe

- The dimensions of the cut vegetables are estimates. It does not have to be accurate as long as it is close. If you want, you can swap the orange or yellow pepper for red. This recipe is quite versatile and could easily be doubled for a large amount.

Nutritional information

- Calories: 111
- Total Fat: 2g
- Saturated Fat: 1g
- Cholesterol: 10mg
- Sodium: 58mg
- Carbohydrates: 19g
- Sugar: 18 g
- Calcium: 15%

Mediterranean Veggie Pita Sandwich

Makes 2 pita bread, can be multiplied for more portions

Time preparation: 4hours: 30mins

Ingredients

- 1/4 cup chopped carrots
- A handful of baby spinach
- 1/4 cup chickpeas
- 1 tsp of crumbled feta cheese
- 2 tsp. of fine chopped sun-dried tomatoes
- 2 teaspoons of chopped kalamata olives
- Season with salt and pepper

Preparation

1. The chopped carrots, baby spinach, chickpeas, crumbled feta cheese, chopped sun-dried tomatoes, chopped kalamata olives, salt and pepper. Spread the bath in every pita pant. Sort the rest of the ingredients between the boxes. Eat immediately or pack in a container for lunch. Cool the device if you prepare it for more than 4 hours before eating.

Nutritional information

- Calories   287.6
- Sodium   716.0 mg
- Potassium   263.6 mg
- Total Carbohydrate   45.7 g
- Dietary Fiber   6.8 g

Pumpkin filled with vegetables and quinoa

Time preparation: 35 minutes

Ingredients

4 portions

- 2 pieces of Italian pumpkin
- 2 tablespoons olive oil
- 1 tablespoon of onion
- Cut 2 pieces of carrots into strips
- In Cut 1 piece of potato into cubes
- Cut 2 pieces of paprika into strips
- 1 cup of cooked quinoa
- 1 teaspoon curry

- Enough of ground bread
- To the taste of salt and pepper

Preparation

1. Preheat the oven to 180 ° C
2. Cut the Italian pumpkin lengthwise and remove the filling place with water in a bowl.
3. Heat over medium heat in a pan, add the oil, quinoa and onion, add the carrots, potatoes and paprika and cook for 3 minutes, season with salt and pepper curry.
4. Put the pumpkins in a tray and fill with the filling, place on the ground bread and bake for 10 minutes.

Nutritional information

- Percent of daily values based on a 2,000 calorie diet.
- calories 232 kcal 12%
- Carbohydrates 40.4 g 13%
- Proteins 8,9 g 18%
- Lipids 3.8 g 5.8%
- Fiber 4.4 g 8.9%
- sugar 0.2 g 0.2%
- Cholesterol 0.0 mg 0.0%

Quinoa confetti

Time preparation: 30 minutes

Ingredients

4 portions

- 1 1/2 cups vegetable stock (low sodium) or water
- 1 cup of well-washed and drained quinoa
- 1/2 teaspoon salt
- 1/2 teaspoon black pepper
- 1 cup of mixed frozen vegetables (e.g carrots, peas, corn, etc.)

Preparation

1. Add the vegetable stock or water in a medium saucepan over medium heat and bring everything to a boil.
2. Add quinoa, salt, and pepper, reduce to low heat and cover the pan with a lid. Cook it until the liquid has evaporated and the quinoa is soft for about 15 minutes. Remove the lid, pour in the vegetables and move it with a fork. Cover again so that the vegetables are cooked with the steam of quinoa.

Nutritional information

Percent of daily values based on a 2,000-calorie diet.

- Calories 268 kcal 13%
- Carbohydrates 45, 3 g 15%
- Proteins 11, 8 g 24%
- Lipids 4, 0 g 6, 1%
- Fiber 7, 4 g 15%
- Sugar 1.2 g 1.3%
- Cholesterol 0, 0 mg 0.0%

Shrimp and Zucchini Skewers

Time preparation: 25 minutes

Ingredients

- Zucchini
- Prawns
- Cold water

Preparation

1. As simple as alternating slices of zucchini rolled with prawns in the middle and roasting on a griddle a couple of minutes per side. So that the zucchini slices do not break when rolled, squeeze them a little first and then pass them through cold water.

Nutritional Information

- Calories 87
- Calories from Fat 13   % Daily Value
- Total Fat 2g2%
- Saturated Fat 1g2%
- Monounsaturated Fat 0g
- Polyunsaturated Fat 0g
- Cholesterol 0mg0%
- Sodium 30mg1%
- Total Carbohydrate 17g6%
- Dietary Fiber 5g22%
- Sugars 13g
- Protein 7g

Thai steak salad with herbs and onions

Time preparation: 25 minutes

Ingredients

For four portion

- One flank or rump steak (600 g)
- Salt
- 1 tbsp. peanut oil
- Two red onions
- 1 piece Ginger (20 g)
- One red chili pepper
- One cucumber
- 3 handful Asian herbs (30 g)
- 1 tbsp. rice vinegar
- 3 tbsps. lime juice
- 2 tbsps. Fish sauce
- 1 tsp. honey

- Paprika
- Chili powder
- Pepper
- meat

Preparation

2. Rinse meat, one flank or rump steak, pat dry and salt. Heat the peanut oil and then fry the steak on both sides for 6-8 minutes over high heat. Remove meat from the frying pan and let it rest.
3. Meanwhile, peel onions and ginger. Halve onions and cut into strips. Chop ginger. Cut chili pepper into half lengthwise remove seeds, wash and cut into fine rings. Clean the cucumber, wash, quarter it and slice it. Wash Asian herbs shake dry and peel off leaves.
4. Add ginger with vinegar, lime juice, fish sauce, honey and 2-3 tablespoons water to a dressing, season it with paprika, chili powder, salt, and pepper.
5. Slice the meat and arrange with herbs, chili rings, cucumber and onions on a plate and drizzle with the dressing.

Nutritional Information

- Calories: 390 kcal

Distinguishing Physical Hunger From The Emotional Hunger In Eating Disorders

In this section study, the definition of intuitive eating behaviors, the factors that contribute to gaining this ability and the importance of using this skill as an intervention technique in the treatment of eating disorders are mentioned. Intuitive eating is the way an individual eats by listening to and adapting to the physical hunger and satiety signals naturally given by his body. In the researches, intuitive eating attitudes and behaviors and body image, physical awareness level, there was a positive relationship between self-perception and life satisfaction levels, but there was a negative relationship between intuitive eating attitudes and behaviors and the tendency to internalize thin body ideal, body mass index and eating disorder symptoms. Considering the results of the studies, it was necessary to develop intervention techniques to gain intuitive eating skills in order to increase the effectiveness of eating disorder treatment. The results of the research support this argument. Intervention programs that support intuitive eating have been found to contribute to the development of healthy eating attitudes and behaviors and to significantly reduce episodes of excessive eating or binge eating.

This section depicts the definition of the term, i.e., intuitive eating, the ways in which they develop the skills. Intuitive eating is known as the ability to respond to one's inner body.

Researches studies indicate that intuitive eating is positively related to body image, self-esteem and satisfaction with life; and is inversely related to internalization of media appearance ideals, body mass index and eating disorder symptomatology. Results highlight the importance of developing intuitive eating intervention programs. Research findings buttress this assumption as studies show that intuitive eating intervention programs encourage the adoption of healthy eating behaviors and significant reduction in binge eating symptoms.

In this study, as a protective factor preventing the occurrence of eating disorders, it is found that the individual has the ability of healthy eating attitudes and behaviors from a young age. Especially in the last two decades, as obesity has increased rapidly in all countries, scientists have argued that research should change direction and emphasize the necessity of studies investigating health-protective behaviors. Therefore, in this guide, the definition of healthy eating attitudes and behaviors, the factors affecting this ability and the importance of using this skill as an intervention technique in the treatment of eating disorders will be included. In 1995, Tribole and Resch developed the concept of intuitive eating based on the philosophy of nutrition in order to define healthy eating attitudes and behaviors. Intuitive eating is the way an individual eats by listening to and adapting to the signals of physical hunger, satiety and satisfaction that the body naturally gives. The concept of intuitive eating is also known in the field of nutrition and dietetics with concepts such as non-diet approach, normal eating, adaptive eating, wisdom eating and conscious eating. Tribole and Resch, in their original name Intuitive eating: A recovery book for chronic dieter, have based the concept of intuitive eating on three basic elements:

1) Unconditional permission to eat (when hungry and desirable)

2) Eating maining for physical reasons rather than emotional reasons 3) relying on the symptoms of physical hunger and satiety when deciding when and how much to eat.

Intuitive Eating

1. Unconditional Permission to Eat (When Hungry and Desired Food): Unconditional permission to eat is defined as eating the desired food when the person feels physical hunger. Individuals who exhibit this type of eating behavior neither try to ignore their physical hunger nor tend to avoid eating unacceptable foods by classifying them as acceptable and unacceptable. Eating behavior of individuals who give them unconditional permission to eat is controlled by physical hunger and satiety signals. Therefore, individuals with such eating behavior do not experience excessive eating behavior.

On the other hand, according to the researches, when, how much and what nutrients put conditions on their food, the feeling of deprivation and the state of the mind is constantly engaged in food. The most striking research to measure the physiological and psychological effects of dietary restriction, in other words, conditional eating behavior, is the Minnesota Starvation Experiment. Keys, Brozek, Henschel, Mickelsen and Taylor (1950), in a study conducted with 36 men aged 22 to 33 years, limited the daily calorie intake of participants to 1560 kilocalories for 6 months. As a result of this strict diet program, it was found that the participants' minds were constantly busy with food and showed binge eating behavior when they stopped dieting.

In the study of Herman and Polivy (1988), it was observed that individuals restricting daily calorie intake exhibited excessive eating behavior as a result of breaking dietary rules or consuming foods that they call forbidden food. They tend to eat, and when they reach physical saturation, they stop eating. These individuals who show eating behavior based on their physical hunger use food as fuel. In contrast, individuals with impaired eating patterns, even though they do not feel physical hunger, they tend to eat to cope with the fluctuations in their mood, and even if they reach physical saturation, they do not stop eating until they reach emotional fullness. These individuals who display eating behavior based on their emotional hunger use food as a tool.

Physical hunger is felt in the lower part of the body and a few hours after eating. Emotional hunger is felt in the upper part of the body and independent of eating times. Physical hunger ends with the body's energy intake. However, emotional hunger, despite the feeling of satiety, ends up with more energy intake than the body needs. Although physical hunger is removed when a feeling of satisfaction occurs, when emotional hunger is relieved, feelings of guilt and embarrassment emerge. Physical Fasting and Toughness

The state of awareness is an innate ability. Birch, Johnson, Andresen, Petersen and Schulte (1991), when examining the eating behavior of children between 2 and 5 years of age, although the amount of food consumed by children varies at a meal, they found that there is no difference between the total amount of calories taken daily. Most caregivers observe the variability in children's eating behavior and conclude that they cannot adequately regulate food intake and adopt compelling strategies to control children's eating behavior. Such strategies are counterproductive, as they impose external rules instead of innate signals of innate hunger and saturation, and lead to a break from internal experience and innate ability to regulate food intake. Indeed, In children who were forced to eat, weight gain, tendency to eat without feeling physical hunger and eating behavior to cope with their emotions were observed. 8 In the study of Faith, Scanlon, Birch, Francis and Sherry (2004), it was found that children whose food intake was restricted by their parents showed eating behavior even though they did not feel physical hunger and body mass indices (BMI) were higher than children whose food intake was not restricted by their parents. It was found that. The philosophy underlying intuitive eating can be summarized as the individual's innate knowledge and awareness of supporting this type of eating, and all he has to do is rely on the physical signals coming from his body. Intuitive eating supports the principle of eating when the abdomen is hungry and stop eating when the abdomen is saturated.

10 Principles of Intuitive Eating

1. Reject Diet Mentality. Throw away diet books and magazines that give you false hopes of losing weight more quickly, easily and permanently. Take a stand against all these diet lies that make you feel unsuccessful when you start a new diet program, but you don't get results or you get all the weight back. If you have any hope of developing a new diet program that will work miracles, this will prevent you from exhibiting intuitive eating attitudes and behaviors.

2. Respect Your Feeling of Hunger. Get enough energy and eat carbohydrates to feed your body biologically. Otherwise, you can trigger over-eating behavior, which is the primitive impulse. When you reach the point of extreme hunger, you will be away from restrained and conscious eating behavior. However, if you respect the feeling of hunger, the biological signal, you will see that your body eats as much as it needs. With this experience, you will regain your confidence in restrained meals.

3. Peace with Food. Declare a truce and put an end to your battle with food! Allow yourself to eat unconditionally. If you stipulate that you should not eat yourself a certain food; this attitude can lead to a feeling of deprivation, which can lead to craving and binge eating behavior that you cannot avoid.

4. Challenge the Food Police. Food Police controls the unreasonable rules created by the diet mindset. Therefore, you must challenge the Food Police, which calls you good for eating under 1000 calories but bad for eating a slice of chocolate cake. By removing Food Police from your life, you will have taken an important step towards regaining your intuitive eating ability.

5. Respect Your Feeling of Toughness. Listen to the body signals that you are no longer hungry. When you reach saturation, observe the symptoms that occur in your body. Take a break into the middle of your meal and question both the taste of the food you eat and the level of saturation you feel at that moment.

6. Discover the Satisfaction Factor. We sometimes ignore feelings of pleasure and satisfaction from the act of eating, which is the most basic gift of our existence. Whereas, when you allow yourself to eat the food you desire at that moment, you will create a attractive and inviting environment for yourself. If you allow this experience, you will see that you have achieved the feeling that you have eaten enough by consuming less food than you anticipated.

7. Feel the Feeling Before You Tend to Eat. Find more effective ways to solve your problems, soothe yourself, feed emotionally, or distract yourself from food. Emotions such as anxiety, loneliness, boredom and anger are feelings that we all experience throughout our lives. Each emotion has its own triggering causes and coping methods. Food, numb our feelings you'll see that you've reached the feeling you've eaten enough, consuming less food than you anticipated.

8. Find more effective ways to solve your problems, soothe yourself, feed emotionally, or distract yourself from food. Emotions such as anxiety, loneliness, boredom and anger are feelings that we all experience throughout our lives. Each emotion has its own triggering causes and coping methods. Food, numb our feelings emotions that we all experience throughout our lives.

9. Rak or by distracting us from our pains, although it gives us a short-term feeling of comfort, it does not help solve the problems we face. In fact, it causes our problems to grow exponentially due to feelings of guilt resulting from excessive eating.

10. Respect Your Body. Accept your genetic structure. Just as a person with shoe size 38 does not have the expectation of entering shoe number 36, the same person should have the same expectation of size. Individuals who have been enslaved to dieting mentality want to have unrealistic body dimensions, so they show an extreme critical approach to their bodies. When you respect the body you have, you love and accept yourself.

Exercise - Feel the Difference. Be active and feel the difference. Change your focus: Instead of you concentrating on the calorie-burning effect of exercise, focus on how you move within your body during exercise. When your goal is to feel good instead of losing weight, you will be more motivated to exercise.

Respect Your Health; Tolerant Nutrition. Make your food choices considering your health and taste. You don't need to go through a unique diet to be healthy. A snack or a meal doesn't put you on weight, nor does it cause nutritional shortages. For a healthy diet, it is sufficient to demonstrate consistent and stable eating attitudes and behaviors.

RESEARCH ON INTUITIVE EATING ATTITUDES AND BEHAVIORS

Scientific research was needed to objectively examine intuitive eating attitudes and behaviors. In order to be used in these scientific studies, it was necessary to develop a scale that graded intuitive eating attitudes and behaviors. Realizing this need, Tracy Tylka developed the Intuitive Eating Scale (IES) in 2006, originally called the Intuitive Eating Scale (IES). When designing the scale, Tracy Tylka was based on the three basic elements mentioned above, developed by Tribole and Resch. In the scale consists of 21 items, Tylka and Kroon Van Diest developed the Intuitive Eating Scale-2 (IES-2) scale. This new scale consists of 23 items; 11 original and 12 new items. The IES-2 scale, unconditional permission to eat, eating based on physical rather than emotional causes, There are 4 sub-tests: relying on physical hunger and satiety symptoms and body-food selection compliance when deciding when and how much to eat. Increasing scores indicate an increase in the tendency to show intuitive eating attitudes and behaviors.

The first study of intuitive eating and attitude behavior was conducted in 2006 by Tylka, who developed the IES scale. In this study, individuals with intuitive eating attitudes and behaviors were found to have high self-esteem and low BMI. It was also found that these individuals were more optimistic and did not tend to internalize the thin body ideal created by contemporary culture. 2 As the result of the research conducted by Madden, Leong, Gray and Horwath (2012); they had low BMI and a 10-point increase in the scale corresponded to a 4.5 kilogram decrease in total weight. Gast, Nielsen, Hunt, and Leiker (2015) found that women with high scores on the IES scale had low BMI and that these women had internal motivation to exercise. August-Horvath and Tylka (2011) found that the acceptance of their bodies by others has a predictive effect on women's appreciation of their bodies and their intuitive eating behavior. Dockendorff, Petrie, Greenlef, and Martin (2012) adapted the IES scale to adolescents and as a result of the study, it was determined that adolescents exhibiting intuitive eating behavior did not tend to internalize low BMI, positive mood and thin body ideal. As a result of Galloway, Farrow and Martz (2010), it was found that university students who had parents who control eating behavior and restrict eating in childhood had higher BMI, exhibited emotional eating behavior and had low scores on IES scale compared to other students. Hawks, Madanat, Hawks and Harris (2005), when examining the effect of intuitive eating on physical health, found that women with intuitive eating behavior, serum triglyceride levels were significantly lower. As a result of this research, it is claimed that intuitive eating behavior has a predictive effect on decreasing the risk of heart diseases.

In summary, in the researches, intuitive eating attitudes and behaviors and body image, physical awareness level, a positive correlation was found between self-perception and life satisfaction levels, however, with intuitive eating attitudes and behaviors.

A negative correlation was found between the tendency to internalize the slim body ideal, BMI and eating disorder symptoms. Considering the results of the studies, it has become important to develop intervention techniques to gain intuitive eating skills in order to increase the effectiveness of eating disorder treatment.

Conclusion

Many studies have shown that sugar affects the brain just as drugs or alcohol do . The "high" that causes refined sugar is followed by an inevitable "downturn", which creates addictive behavior. We always want more, we cannot limit ourselves to "a little", and we must continue eating them with the consequent impact on our diet and health. The same goes for processed flours. The bread of hamburgers, pastries, pizzas. We eat everything in excess. How you eat will usually give you an idea of what your body asks you. However, the habit and eating different things makes your body "forget" the nutrients it needs, weakening your health. If you do not give your body the necessary nutrients through a balanced diet, it will not ask you for such nutrients by not eating them regularly. Your body asks you what it knows.